BLOODSUCKERS
OF THE ANIMAL WORLD

by Jody Sullivan Rake

Content Consultant:
David Stephens, PhD
Professor of Ecology, Evolution, and Behavior
University of Minnesota

Reading Consultant:
Barbara J. Fox
Professor Emerita
North Carolina State University

CAPSTONE PRESS
a capstone imprint

Blazers Books are published by Capstone Press,
1710 Roe Crest Drive, North Mankato, Minnesota 56003
www.capstonepub.com

Library of Congress Cataloging-in-Publication Data

Rake, Jody Sullivan, author.
  Bloodsuckers of the animal world / by Jody Sullivan Rake.
      pages cm. — (Disgusting creature diets)
  Summary: "Discusses various organisms throughout the world that consume blood as a part of their diets"—
Provided by publisher.
  Includes bibliographical references and index.
  ISBN 978-1-4914-1997-7 (library binding)
  ISBN 978-1-4914-2174-1 (eBook pdf)
  1. Bloodsucking animals—Juvenile literature. 2. Bloodsucking insects—Juvenile literature. I. Title.
  QL756.55.R35 2015
  591.5'3—dc23   2014023798

Editorial Credits
Abby Colich, editor; Kyle Grenz, designer; Jo Miller, media researcher;
Katy LaVigne, production specialist

Photo Credits
Clinton Bauder, 28-29; Dreamstime: Deyangeorgiev, cover (skin), Joao Estevao Andreade De Freitas, 6-7; Getty
Images: De Agostini/Archivio B, 20-21, Oxford Scientific/Roger Eritja, 22-23; Minden Pictures: Jim Clare, 10-11;
Newscom: Danita Delimont Photography/Pete Oxford, 12-13, Minden Pictures/Stephen Dalton, 9, Photoshot/
NHPA/Agence Nature, 15, Photoshot/NHPA/Image Quest 3-D, 24, Photoshot/NHPA/Roger Tidman, 16-17;
Photoshot: NHPA/Paulo de Oliveira, 14; Shutterstock: Henrik Larsson, 25, Kokhanchikov, 4-5, LauraD, 29 (inset),
smuay, 18-19; SuperStock: Biosphoto, 26-27, Minden Pictures, cover (bugs)

Printed in China by Nordica.
1014/CA21401515
092014   008470NORDS15

TABLE OF CONTENTS

REAL VAMPIRES

All animals must eat to survive. Some animal **diets** are unusual. Others are disgusting! Blood is a part of many animal diets.

diet—what an animal eats

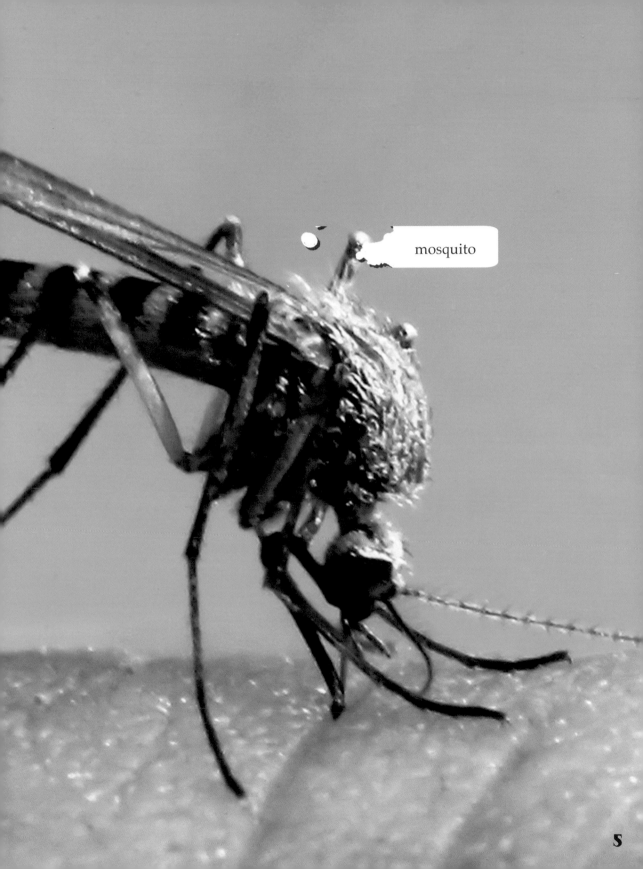

mosquito

Bloodsuckers are **parasites**. Most bloodsuckers don't harm their **hosts**. Hosts that are not harmed can make more blood. Why eat blood? It has a lot of **protein** and **iron**. Animals need protein and iron to live and grow.

parasite—an animal or plant that lives on or inside another animal or plant
host—an animal from which a parasite feeds
protein—a nutrient that builds muscle and strength
iron—a mineral found in blood

Fact!
Many bloodsuckers have special spit. The spit helps keep the host's blood flowing. This means more dinner for the bloodsucker.

tick

I WANT TO BITE YOUR ANKLE!

Vampire bats live in Mexico and Central and South America. They earn their name! These bats sleep all day. Then they come out at night to hunt. Vampire bats are the only **mammals** that eat only blood.

Fact!
The common vampire bat sucks blood from cows, pigs, and horses. The hairy-legged and white-winged vampire bats eat bird blood.

mammal—an animal with hair or fur that gives birth to young and feeds them milk

Vampire bats don't usually bite
necks. The common vampire bat
finds food during flight. It lands
near a sleeping animal. Then it
crawls close enough to make a
small bite in the ankle and lick
up the blood.

BLOODThIRSTY BIRD

Finches are songbirds that eat seeds. When
seeds are scarce, a vampire finch eats blood.
It climbs on the back of a bird
called a booby and pecks at
the booby's neck. Then the
finch sucks blood from
the tiny wound.

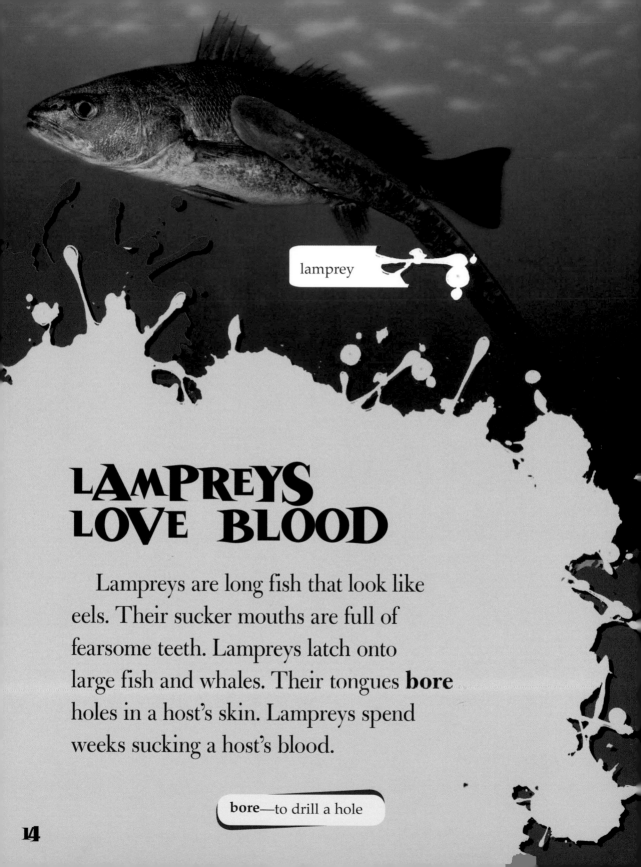

lamprey

LAMPREYS LOVE BLOOD

Lampreys are long fish that look like eels. Their sucker mouths are full of fearsome teeth. Lampreys latch onto large fish and whales. Their tongues **bore** holes in a host's skin. Lampreys spend weeks sucking a host's blood.

bore—to drill a hole

Fact!

Lampreys are one of the few bloodsuckers that can kill their hosts. Many hang on until their victims die.

THE CREEPY CANDIRU

The tiny candiru fish is the size of a toothpick. This little bloodsucker swims into the gills of a larger fish. The candiru finds a **blood vessel** inside its host. Then it settles in for a nice long suck.

blood vessel—a thin tube that carries blood through the body

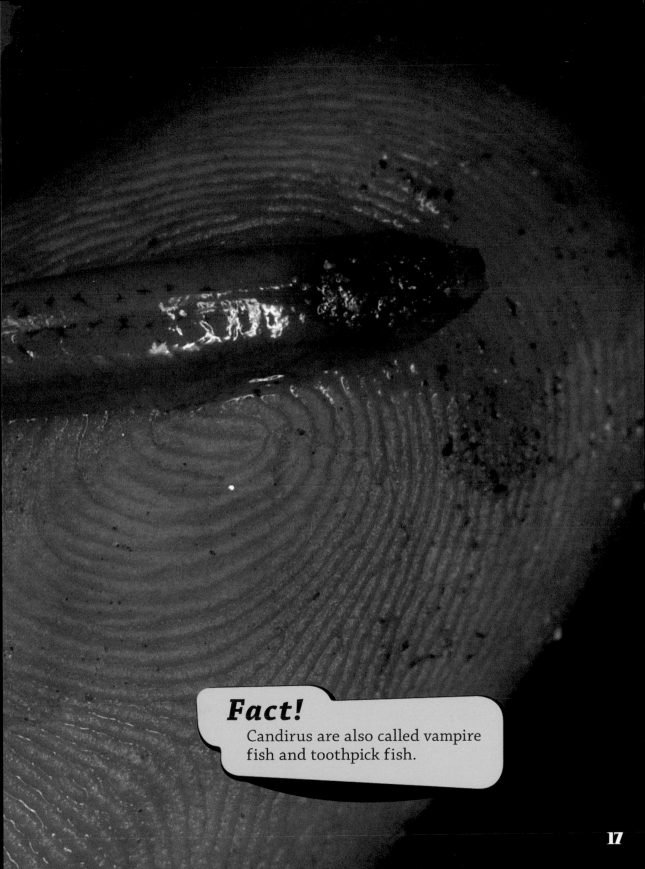

Fact!
Candirus are also called vampire fish and toothpick fish.

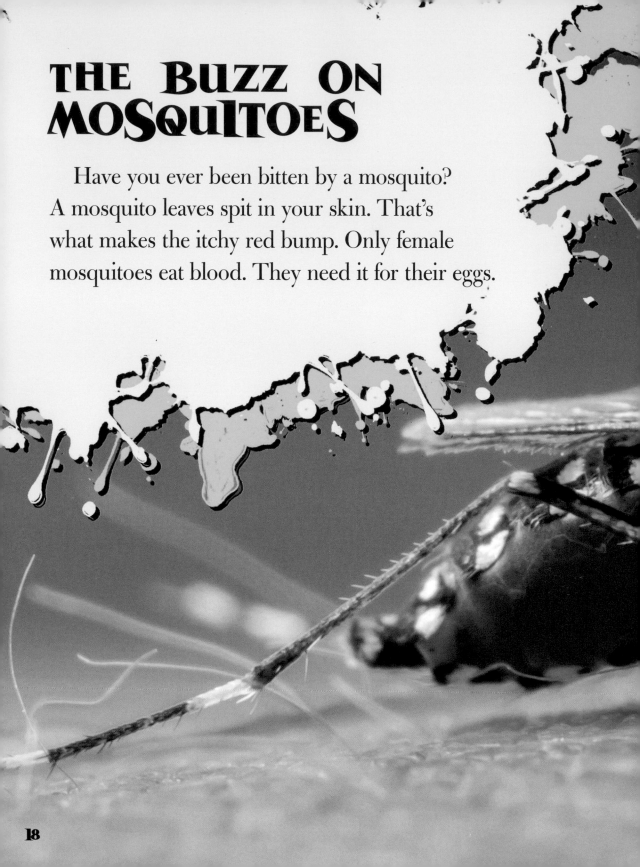

THE BUZZ ON MOSQUITOES

Have you ever been bitten by a mosquito? A mosquito leaves spit in your skin. That's what makes the itchy red bump. Only female mosquitoes eat blood. They need it for their eggs.

repellent—a substance that keeps something unwanted away

PARASITE MOTH

Most moths are harmless **nectar** eaters.
The male vampire moth of Siberia is
different. Blood is the favorite food of
this vampire moth. It uses an extra-long,
sharp tongue for poking animal skin and
gulping blood!

nectar—a sweet liquid found in many flowers

GOOD NIGHT! SLEEP TIGHT!

A bed bug looks like an apple seed. It hides in furniture, carpet, and even books. This bloodsucker sleeps during the day. It comes out at night to bite and suck its host's blood.

Fact!

You won't feel a bed bug bite. Its spit will **numb** your skin before it bites.

numb—to take away feeling

BUGGED BY BUGS

Many bugs are bloodsuckers.
Fleas feast on the blood of animals
such as dogs and cats. Ticks dine
on the blood of deer and other animals.
They bite humans too. Be careful!
Like mosquitoes, some ticks spread diseases.

flea

tick

Fact!

Some ticks hang on to a twig or blade of
grass for weeks. They wait for a victim to
come by and then latch on to their host.

DISGUSTING BUT HELPFUL

Leeches are related to earthworms.
Leeches live in lakes, rivers, and ponds.
A leech has a suction cup on each end
of its body. Both ends hold on while
one end does the sucking.

Fact!

Doctors have used leeches for thousands of years. Today doctors use leeches to increase blood flow in some patients. Leeches help heal damaged areas of the human body.

A FuSSY BLOODSuCKING SNAIL

The Cooper's nutmeg snail eats the blood of only one animal—the electric ray. The snail can smell the ray from 75 feet (23 meters) away. It sticks its long, bloodsucking tongue into the bottom of the ray.

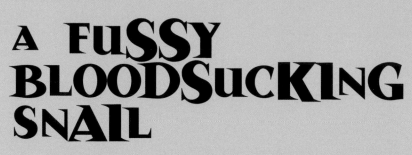

electric ray

Fact!

If there are no electric rays around, the Cooper's nutmeg snail stays buried in the ocean floor. It can go up to 12 days without eating.

GLOSSARY

blood vessel (BLUHD VE-suhl)—a thin tube that carries blood through the body

bore (BOR)—to drill a hole

diet (DY-uht)—what an animal eats

host (HOHST)—an animal from which a parasite feeds

iron (EYE-urn)—a mineral found in blood

mammal (MAM-uhl)—an animal with hair or fur that gives birth to young and feeds them milk

nectar (NEK-tur)—a sweet liquid found in many flowers

numb (NUM)—to take away feeling

parasite (PAIR-uh-site)—an animal or plant that lives on or inside another animal or plant

protein (PROH-teen)—a nutrient that builds muscle and strength

repellent (ri-PEL-uhnt)—a substance that keeps something unwanted away

READ MORE

Knapp, Ron. *Bloodsucking Creatures.* Bizarre Science. Berkeley Heights, N.J.: Enslow Publishers, 2011.

Rodger, Ellen. *Bloodsucking Lice and Fleas.* Creepy Crawlies. New York: Crabtree Publishing, 2010.

INTERNET SITES

FactHound offers a safe, fun way to find Internet sites related to this book. All of the sites on FactHound have been researched by our staff.

Here's all you do:

Visit *www.facthound.com*

Type in this code: 9781491419977

Check out projects, games and lots more at
www.capstonekids.com

InDex